Contents

Early life 4

Nursing the sick 6

Wishing and hoping 8

Nurse Nightingale 10

'The Lady with the Lamp' 12

A national hero 14

Changes in nursing 16

Paintings 18

Photographs...20

Museums and artefacts 22

Glossary...24

Index 24

Any words appearing in the text in bold, **like this**, are explained in the Glossary.

Early life

Florence Nightingale was born in 1820. Her parents were visiting Florence, in Italy. She was named after the city. Florence had one older sister called Parthenope. They lived with their parents.

Florence and her sister with their parents.

Florence

Parthenope

Florence's father

Florence

Florence's father taught her foreign languages, history and mathematics.

Florence's parents were very rich. Like many rich girls of the time, Florence did not go to school. But she was a good **student**.

Nursing the sick

Florence's childhood was happy. As she grew older, her parents thought she should find a rich young man and settle down as a wife and mother.

Florence went to wonderful balls like this when she was a young woman.

Florence realized that what she wanted was to nurse the sick. At the time, nurses were often **uneducated** old women. They were nothing like Florence!

Florence's parents would not allow her to become a nurse.

Florence's father

Florence's mother

Wishing and hoping

Florence read all she could about health and hospitals. She became an **expert** on how to keep people healthy and make them better when they became ill.

Florence studied lots of **reports** on health and hospitals.

reports

When she was 30, Florence went to Germany with some friends. She visited a nursing institute at Kaiserswerth. This was where she wanted to study!

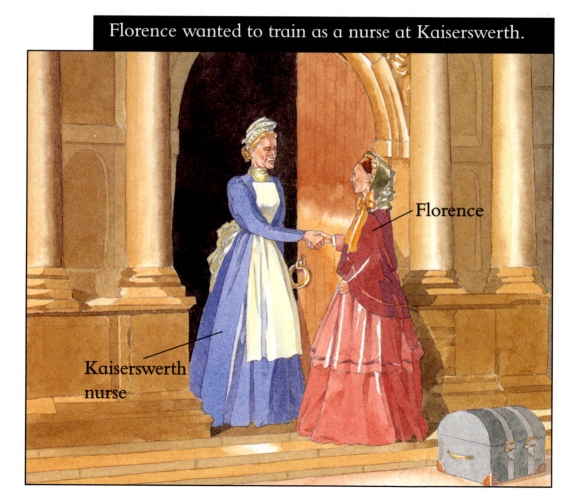

Florence wanted to train as a nurse at Kaiserswerth.

Kaiserswerth nurse

Florence

Nurse Nightingale

In 1851 Florence's parents finally allowed her to go to Kaiserswerth. She also went to Paris, in France, to work as a nurse.

In 1854 Florence heard about the bad conditions for soldiers injured in the **Crimean War** between Britain and Russia. She had to do something.

Florence reading newspaper **reports** about the injured soldiers.

newspaper

Florence

11

'The Lady with the Lamp'

Most injured soldiers were sent to Scutari in Turkey. Florence gathered together supplies and a group of nurses. They travelled to Scutari Hospital.

Florence and a group of nurses set sail for the Crimea.

nurses

Florence

wounded soldier

Florence

lamp

Florence was known as 'The Lady with the Lamp'.

The men called Florence 'The Lady with the Lamp' because she walked around the hospital every night comforting **patients**.

Before Florence arrived, more men were dying from infections than from battle wounds so she made sure they had clean wards and better food.

A national hero

When the war ended in 1856, Florence was famous. In 1860 Florence set up the Nightingale School for Nurses in London.

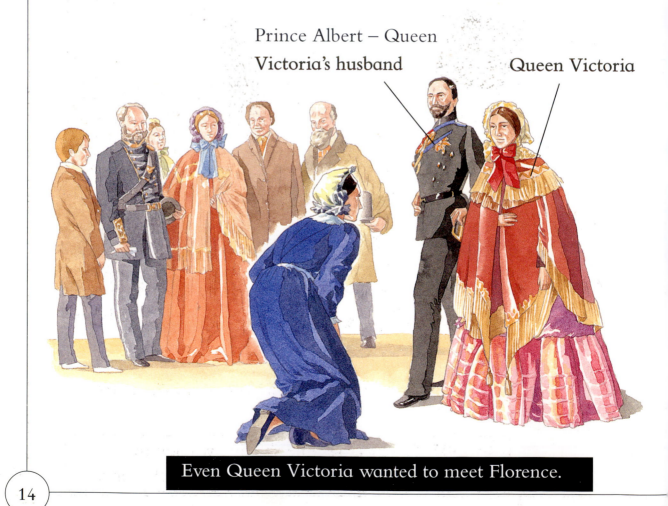

Prince Albert – Queen Victoria's husband

Queen Victoria

Even Queen Victoria wanted to meet Florence.

Florence

Florence gave advice about hospitals and health even from her sick bed.

Everyone wanted Florence's help and advice about hospitals and health. During her life nursing had become a **respected profession**. She died in 1910.

In 1907, Florence became the first woman to receive a special award called the Order of Merit.

Changes in nursing

Two hundred years ago there were no proper nurses to look after sick and injured people.

Many people did not expect to get better in hospitals like these. Can you read what it says on the wall at the end of this ward?

Hospitals were often crowded, noisy and dirty places.

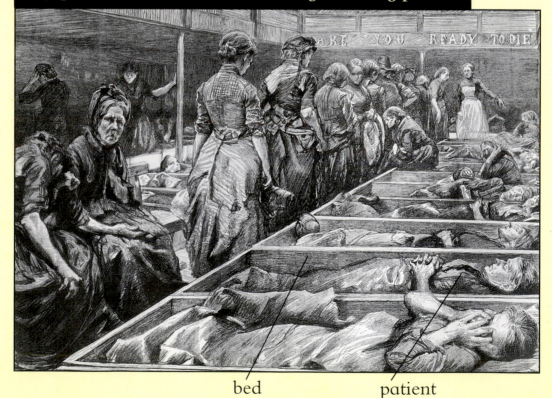

bed   patient

Today **patients** in hospitals are looked after by trained nurses. One reason for this is the hard work and **dedication** of Florence Nightingale.

doctor   nurses

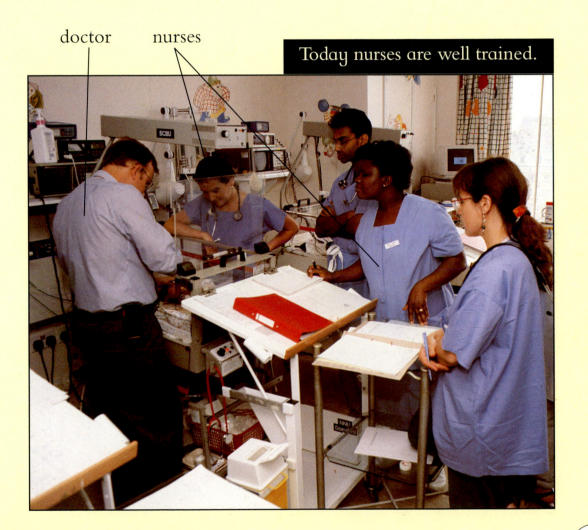

Today nurses are well trained.

Paintings

We can find out more about Florence Nightingale by looking at pictures. This painting shows Florence sitting with her sister, Parthenope.

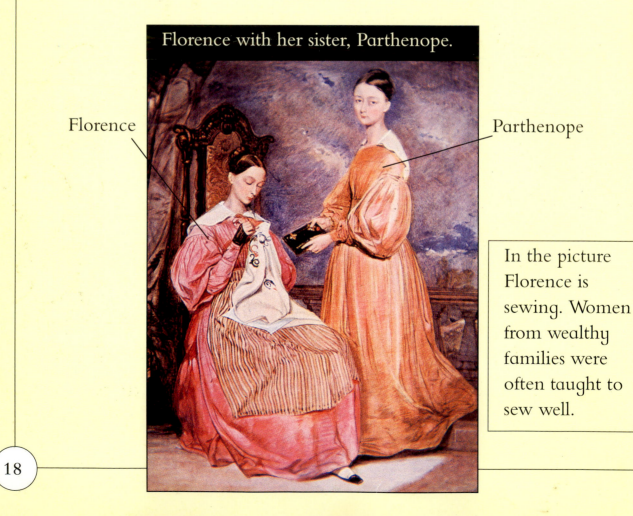

Florence with her sister, Parthenope.

Florence

Parthenope

In the picture Florence is sewing. Women from wealthy families were often taught to sew well.

nurse

wounded
soldier

Florence

Florence in the Scutari Barracks Hospital

Here is a painting of Florence when she was about 35 years old. She is in a **ward** of the Barracks Hospital at Scutari.

Photographs

Here is Florence with a group of nurses from the Nightingale School for Nurses at St Thomas's Hospital in London. It was the first time that nurses had been trained in a hospital.

Florence

Florence with nurses from the Nightingale School for Nurses.

Florence never stopped working, even though she was ill for nearly 50 years. For the last ten years of her life she was blind.

Florence contracted fever in the Crimea and almost died. Her health never recovered from this.

This photograph shows Florence at work.

letters

Museums and artefacts

In London there is a Florence Nightingale Museum. It contains **artefacts** from Florence's life.

Look carefully at the picture on the writing box. It shows Florence and her nurses landing in France on their way to the Crimea.

Here are Florence's writing box, watch, ink and pen.

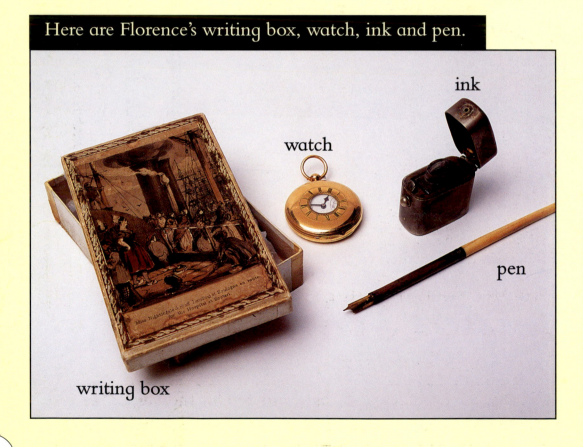

ink

watch

pen

writing box

lamp

Florence's lamp.

Florence used this lamp to visit sick soldiers. She did this in the hospital **wards** at Scutari during the **Crimean War**.

One of the first things Florence ordered for the hospital at Scutari was lots of scrubbing brushes because it was so dirty!

Glossary

This glossary explains difficult words, and helps you to say words which may be hard to say.

artefact thing which people make and use. We can learn about the past by looking at old artefacts. You say *arty-fact*.

Crimean War (1854–1856) fought in an area on the Black Sea, in the south-east of what is now the Ukraine. You say *cry-me-un*.

dedication doing something with total love and devotion

expert someone who knows a lot about a particular subject

patient person who is being treated by a doctor for injuries or a disease

profession job where there are special studies or exams to pass before you can do it

report information gathered together about a subject

respected someone or something that people think is important and valuable

student person who studies

uneducated someone who has not been to school

ward large, open room with many beds, found in hospitals

Index

birth 4

Crimean War 11, 23

death 15

hospitals 8, 10, 12, 13, 15, 16, 17, 19, 20, 23

illness 8, 10, 16, 21, 23

Kaiserswerth 9, 10

photographs 17, 20, 21, 22, 23

Queen Victoria 14

school 5, 14, 20

Scutari 12, 19, 23